THE TRUTH ABOUT MUSIC LESSONS

THE TRUTH ABOUT MUSIC LESSONS

The Top 10 Music Lesson Myths...

STEPHAN HUME

Littleton School of Music
and Parker Music Academy

THE TRUTH ABOUT MUSIC LESSONS
The Top Ten Music Lesson Myths . . . Busted

ISBN (paperback): 978-1-964046-97-6
ISBN (ebook): 979-8-90343-060-4

Expert Press
11610 Pleasant Ridge Rd.
Suite 103, #189
Little Rock, AR 72223
www.ExpertPress.net

Copyediting by Wendy Lukasiewicz
Proofreading by Abby Kendall
Text and cover design and composition by Paperback Expert

With gratitude in my heart,
I dedicate this book—as well as all creative
endeavors and the inspiration received from
countless students, staff, and families—to God.

CONTENTS

FOREWORD

When I was a kid, I took piano lessons. I didn't have much choice in the matter—my mom was a very good amateur piano player, and my sister and I were going to learn to play. I think many kids have had the same experience: spending an hour each week learning scales, exercises, and short songs ("Little Brown Jug," anyone?) meant to teach the fundamentals of reading music and playing an instrument.

If this method actually engaged kids, most of us wouldn't have quit at the first opportunity! I know I did—mainly because I didn't have anything personally invested in those lessons or my practice sessions at home. It all felt like homework instead of something creative or enjoyable.

Years later, when my own daughter expressed an interest in learning to play first the piano and later the guitar, I hoped for something that would "stick" a little more than my childhood experience. What I wanted for her was simple: I wanted her to love music. I wanted her to feel that spark of excitement when she figured out how to play a song she loved, and to carry that joy with her for life. Of course, I understood the importance of learning the fundamentals, but I didn't want those fundamentals to become barriers that drained the fun out of learning.

Enter Littleton School of Music.

What intrigued me most was the idea that my daughter, Sarah, would be able to make a list of songs she liked—songs that meant something to her—and her teacher would use those to teach her the basics. No, she couldn't jump right in and learn Beethoven's *Moonlight Sonata* (something she wanted to play because my mom used to perform it for her), but she could start with some Katy Perry or other pop songs she loved. From there, her teacher helped her connect the dots between the music she enjoyed and the fundamentals she needed to know—matching notes from the sheet music to piano keys or learning the guitar chords that brought her favorite songs to life.

Because she was working on music she genuinely enjoyed, Sarah was enthusiastic about practicing outside of lessons. She loved being able to play along with her favorite songs as she improved, and lessons became something she looked forward to rather than something she had to endure.

Most importantly, her time at the school wasn't about rote memorization or perfection. It was about having fun, building confidence, and deepening her love for music. It didn't matter that she couldn't recite a piece of music note for note—what mattered was that she was developing a lifelong relationship with creativity, learning, and joy.

Looking back, I realize how different my own experience might have been if I had learned in an environment like this—one that nurtured curiosity and self-expression instead of focusing solely on drills and technique. The approach that Littleton School of Music takes—meeting students where they are, tapping into what excites them, and building skill through joy—is exactly what keeps kids engaged and helps them grow, not just as musicians but as people.

If you're a parent considering music lessons for your child, I hope this book encourages you to think differently about what those lessons can be. Music isn't just something to be mastered; it's something to be *loved*. And that's exactly what my daughter found through this school.

—Cathy Mueller
(Regular person—just like you)

PREFACE

Who Makes These Things Up?

One of the most successful television shows of all time was *MythBusters*. If you ever watched it, you were one of many people whose eyes were glued to the screen as you witnessed a team of daredevils testing popular "myths"—whether hammers smashed together would shatter with deadly force, whether a jawbreaker would explode in the microwave, whether using your cell phone while pumping gas would cause an explosion.

MythBusters was great entertaining fun, of course. But there was also a big element of curiosity that helped make the show so popular. We really wanted to know if those myths were true—or not.

Myths exist in society for many reasons, some of them good reasons. Some myths are "true," or real, or at least based on reality. That's good. "Safety first," right? If using your cell phone at the gas pump really can blow you to kingdom come, you would want to know that. Some myths have some element of true danger to them. For example, I don't recommend standing underneath a skyscraper while someone drops a penny from the seventieth floor, just to see what would happen.

But in many cases, myths have a reputation of being false, like old wives' tales (to borrow from *Harry Potter and the Deathly Hallows*). That's because, let's face it, many myths are totally false.

Who makes these things up?

* * *

What does all of this have to do with music lessons? After all, you didn't pick up this book because you were curious about microwaving jawbreakers or because you wanted a refresher on your favorite episodes of *MythBusters*. You likely picked it up because you're curious about music lessons. But you've heard, or at least heard implied, that "music lessons don't make sense unless you're really talented" or that "you have to know how to read music in order to play it."

If you can relate to statements like these, this is the book for you. Because in the course of running music schools for about two decades, employing dozens of music teachers, and operating a business that's delivered hundreds of lessons to hundreds of students, I've likely heard them all. I've compiled an extensive list of the myths people have come to believe about music lessons. It's a bit like a standard frequently asked questions list. However (spoiler alert!), these myths are all debunked—or *busted*—on a regular basis.

It turns out that music lessons transcend the assumptions about, and appeal of, almost all other extracurricular activities, including sports and martial arts. To become a star quarterback, for instance, you have to be able to read a defense without sounding out the linebackers. But (another spoiler alert) you do not have to be able to read music in order for music lessons to make a big, positive difference in your life. And that's just one example.

Primarily, I've assembled this material as a resource to help parents, teachers, and families. Here, you'll learn that the myths or misconceptions that may have held you back from making music lessons a powerful blessing in your family (particularly in the life of your kids) are just not true. We're going to bust those myths, one at a time. And it's going to be far safer (and far more appropriate) than any experiments you may have seen on television. No flashy cameras, no bullets, no explosions, no injuries of any kind. Instead, you'll find that the experiments testing these music lesson myths have all been done before, countless times, by loving parents who had to overcome their initial skepticism in order to feel comfortable enrolling their kids in music lessons.

If you're like me, you understand that the one thing that binds us together as parents is our love for our children.

We would do anything for them! So as you turn these pages, I invite you to keep an open mind to what we've learned through many years of trial and error (and a bit of humor). This collection is informed by hundreds of reviews, conversations, and comment cards from folks like you who had the same questions regarding things they had heard about music lessons. Really, it's not just me. You're going to read about the myth-busting experiences of hundreds of other students (and their families). You can trust that they've tested these myths for you.

Hopefully, you'll also enjoy a laugh or two while you pick up some practical facts that will help you and your family get the most out of learning to make music.

My promise to you is simple: After reading these chapters, you'll have a much better understanding of what you should expect before, during, and after music lessons have become part of your family's life. I bust these myths in no particular order. In fact, I've cut out a handful of them so that this book can be limited to the most impactful myths that might be holding you back from the incredible blessing music lessons can be.

Entertainment aside, it means a lot to me that you get great value out of reading this book. After all, music is one of the cheapest forms of therapy and one of the highest forms of expression. And that's what I want for your child, and for your entire family.

INTRODUCTION

My Story, and the Start of
Our First Music School

A fourteen-year-old came into the lesson room with a guitar in one hand and only one eye visible. The other eye was hidden behind a long pile of hair intentionally covering half his face. He was dressed all in black, including a pair of gloves that showed the ends of his fingertips. He didn't smile, but he walked with intention. His parents had signed him up for music lessons as a last resort. Nothing else was working. They couldn't reach him. They confided in me that they felt their son was truly lost. And, honestly, he did have that look about him.

When his folks walked away and I was left with the young man, what I saw was myself, at least the kid I had been years before. Yes, there was a period of my own life that was filled with a lot of sadness. A lot of turmoil at home. In writing this, I was tempted to go into great detail about what life looked like for me at that age. But I took a lot of that stuff out, because this book isn't meant to bring you down. True, I made some poor choices, like cutting holes in my clothes, hanging out with the wrong kind of kids, and even trying to run away at one point. A lot of the time, I just wanted to hide. In many ways, considering the decisions I made and the terrible decisions people around me made over the years, it's a miracle I'm alive.

When I was twelve years old, I found the guitar. Suddenly, I didn't want to hide any longer. Something lit up inside me, and it still hasn't been extinguished. Some might call it God-given inspiration. Others might say it's the healing power of music. However you look at it, I was just like this black-clad, face-hiding kid who had walked into my music lesson room. Like him, I had probably looked for all the world like a lost cause before I found music. Or maybe music found me.

When he clicked open his guitar case and pulled out his black guitar—shaped like a battle axe—I knew we were going to have some fun. Even if he didn't know it yet. And I correctly guessed that his days of hiding himself were on their way out.

Music Sees You

Music "sees you" when no one else does. Music has a power nothing else has to help you express yourself. They say there are two universal languages: math and music. You don't have to speak the language of music to enjoy it. About that language, famed bassist Victor Wooten is said to have once remarked, "You don't need to know the rules behind it to speak it." (Look him up!)

There's something deep about being able to connect with people when you know you truly have a way to do it. I'm no psychologist, and I'm never going to be a qualified therapist, but I know one thing: When someone has a guitar in their hand, or their fingers on a piano keyboard, or their lips to a vocal microphone, things change . . . Music adds the full worth to our internal sense of joy and light in a way almost nothing else can.

Music changes things for you. Since 2006, we've set out to help make those changes for everyone we can. Whether you come to music lessons from a troubled place of feeling worthless and unseen, or from a more pleasant place of doing well but seeking to squeeze every drop of joy out of life that you can, music lifts you up. We know this—because countless parents and families have told us so.

Over the course of years of music lessons, this is what happened for that lost young man. For one thing, within a few months, he decided it would be okay to show his full face. Meanwhile, he learned all the incredible riffs, from the Deftones to Metallica. He even explored classical music and bought an acoustic guitar. As the years went by, his parents became less and less concerned as they dropped him off at our school, and more and more joyful as they picked him up. He played recitals. He performed in rock shows. And along the way, he began to display new aspects of who he truly was—wonderful attributes we had never seen before.

I'll never forget the day his parents approached me after one of his concerts. "Thank you for all you've done," his mom said, tears in her eyes. "Music completely transformed our son. It brought him back to us!"

I told her I would always remember their son, and their whole family.

What a gift. And here I am, sharing that gift with you.

Is there a story like this in your family's life? Do you know somebody who could really use something special in their life—something they can't find anywhere else? Are you like me, in that hearing stories like this makes you emotional?

There are lots of stories like this, not just among the families who have joined our schools, but all over the world. Right now, people's lives are being transformed by music.

We've seen dozens of students come through our music lesson rooms and finally find an identity. If that sounds like someone you know, then you're on the right track with choosing music for them in their life. But it's important to note that music isn't just for people who need to turn their life around, like the young man described here. People of almost all walks of life, in any situation, will experience music as transformative beyond description.

How It All Started

Many people have asked me how we decided to start our music school. And since you've asked nicely, I'll tell you.

In 2006, I met an investor. I was working at a retail music store, and we met as I was selling him a guitar for his fifteen-year-old son. After many conversations about the transformative power of music, we decided the energy was just right, and we made plans to start a Colorado-based rock music school for kids. Since that time, many things have happened within the structure of our business. We have evolved to teaching many more instruments and styles. But one thing has remained the same for me. Every day, I wake up with an immense sense of responsibility.

Today, we employ dozens of teachers, office staff, and managers, and we continue to be pushed to offer the best experience possible. This book is designed to help you get a grasp of music lessons before you choose where you go. It means a lot to me that you find the right place.

Since we started our school in 2006, it has been almost twenty years (at the time of writing) that we have been running music schools in Colorado. We have made it through changes in ownership, branding, style, location, and not to mention the pandemic year 2020, which left many music schools with no choice but to close. Yet because of wonderful staff, determination, and people like you, we are honored to still be serving our community.

If your family lives near any of our music schools, I would be dishonest if I didn't tell you that I would try to convince you to join us. We're a fantastic option, and our reputation shows it. But my hope is that anyone who decides to take lessons with us will have a meaningful experience, no matter how you arrived at the decision that our schools are the place for you and your family.

Like you, I'm a parent. My wife and I have young children. As is the case with many families these days, our kids participate in many different activities. Recently, I asked my wife about our oldest daughter's pastimes.

"Hey, honey," I said, though Honey is not her real name, "if you had to pull our oldest daughter from one of her activities, which would it be?" She answered immediately. I asked her why that activity came so suddenly to her mind, and she said, "I guess it's because that place doesn't communicate with me very much."

That was an eye-opener for me. I know my daughter enjoys that activity. But it means a lot to my wife that those who run the activity don't communicate more. Duly noted!

That brings up my challenge in presenting this material for you. The myths I'll be busting in the next chapters will mostly be about music. But some of them will have to do with your experience as a customer as well. When you sign your kid up for any sort of activity, a big part of that for you as a parent is how the company organizes things. Your kid can be having a great time in soccer, but if they have a terrible coach, well, you know it won't be as great an experience as it should be. We can enroll our kids in karate, but if the martial arts school never answers their phones, again, you see where I'm heading. It all has to work for you.

I'm aware of the exposure I'm accepting in promising to bust these myths. For one thing, we at our schools have to continue being as excellent as we can be. But I hope you hear in the tone of this writing, and learn from researching us online, that you can conclude that we're a great option to help you and/or your child gain inspiration in life.

In 2026, we'll celebrate our twentieth year in operation. Most music schools don't last that many years before they have to close their doors. Music school owners will tell you it's a tough business. I enjoy telling you about our longevity because I hope it gives you a sense of credibility. But there's danger there. If we act like we know it all or like we have it all figured out, well, then we'll be just like anyone else. And we don't want to be just like anyone else. Because neither are you! You are unique. And so is your kid. So we have to continue to adapt, grow, and learn what works and what doesn't.

I hope you enjoy reading this book. Even if you haven't considered learning to play a musical instrument yourself, I highly recommend it, even if not in lessons. The simple joy of being able to play music is incomparable. You gain a stake of ownership in the music you've always loved. That's a gift no one can ever take away from you.

Who knew that picking up a guitar would be the tiny seed that grew into the giant oak tree in my heart today.

The twelve-year-old version of Stephan who first plucked that string, just trying to tune it, had no idea what was ahead. That first pluck would become the starting point of so many incredible experiences.

Since pouring myself into music that day, I've found myself in some wonderful (and unexpected) places and situations. I've played with some of the best musicians in the world, but I've also learned to play—*joyfully*—with anyone of any skill level who's excited to make music.

I've written dozens of songs, instrumental and vocal, and released music online that has reached people all over the world.

I've been hired for studio projects by dozens of artists who wanted to include my unique style of playing or singing in their music.

I was invited to participate in the world's largest guitar lesson as a shot at the *Guinness Book of World Records*.

I've performed in dozens of venues, from cozy little coffee shops to the iconic Red Rocks Amphitheatre.

I've been honored to play nearly two hundred weddings, corporate events, and private parties.

I've written music for cruise ships.

I've contributed to music publications as an expert on young musical talent, which eventually led to being featured on MTV in a show focusing on young talent.

I've received international awards as both a music school owner and, more generally, as a business owner.

I was honored as a finalist in the Guitars on Fire competition, years ago.

I've led organizations at the forefront of our local business community.

I even got to open in performance for Tommy Emmanuel and Joe Satriani—two of the best guitarists anywhere, and guys I've always admired.

Today, I operate two music schools that serve hundreds of families every week. Historically, we've served thousands. And over the years, I've had the privilege of employing hundreds of music teachers in our community.

Music has brought me so much joy and so many unforgettable opportunities, and I feel like I'm just getting started. I continue to write, perform, and pursue bigger venues, not only because it fills me up but because it gives me a chance to share that joy with others.

I can honestly say that same passion lives on throughout our music schools. I love seeing the live reactions of students and parents, from those learning to play for the first time, to hearing about the accolades students have earned in their own right. I've seen our students go on to create wonderful, meaningful music and projects of their own. I've employed teachers who have toured with some of the biggest names in the music industry.

I'm sharing all these successes to make a point: You never really know. You never know where music might take you or your aspiring youngster.

MYTH NO. 1

Music Lessons Are About Playing the Right Notes

As I write this, our third child is back at the house, busy at her day job, which is learning how to talk.

She's only a year old, so she's got the typical lineup of hilarious things a toddler can say. Every time she tries to say "snack," it sounds like "sah." Her version of "okay" is "otay." And when I told her the other day that hitting her brother wasn't funny, she disagreed with a defiant smile, saying, "Sunny!" Yes, Daddy, it actually *is* funny.

I tried not to spit out my coffee.

As a side note, it's hard as a parent not to laugh when you're trying to correct your children and teach them to have good character, especially when what they're doing is both cute and inappropriate. If you are a parent reading this, you know exactly what I mean. Chances are, no matter who you are, you've experienced this while watching a young child do what they do best: learning about life, while also being cute.

Imagine if, instead of laughing when my child said the wrong word, I pointed my finger in her face disappointingly. Imagine if every time she said something cute (but wrong) or did something hilarious (but inappropriate), my wife and I scowled and told her she's not getting it right. *Maybe she's not talented enough to speak English. Maybe we should try having her learn a simpler language, or maybe she shouldn't talk at all. This is clearly not working.*

Everybody I know would think we aren't fit to be parents if that's how we approached our children's efforts to learn how to talk. So what do we do instead? We laugh. Why? Because it's cute. Because we adore watching our kids learn to form speech, even if what comes out is "wrong" at first. Especially when what comes out is completely wrong or inappropriate. It's "sunny" because we know where they're headed and because they're small and cute. They get automatic patience from everyone because everyone knows that they're learning to speak for the first time. Come to think of it, my folks have told me about some hilarious stuff I said when I was first learning to speak.

A common misconception about music lessons is that, somehow, parents should have an opposite reaction to their kid's learning process. That's the first myth we'll bust: Music lessons are only about playing the right notes.

It's the idea that if a new music student doesn't come home and immediately sing or play the correct notes, the music lessons aren't working. *She did learn to speak English, after all, but maybe she isn't cut out for music. It's not worth the time.*

When the child picks up on this attitude from their parents (and they always do), then they also believe that they aren't cut out for music lessons. It becomes a self-fulfilling prophecy.

Busted: Learning Music Is Like Any Other Learning Process

What if I told you that learning to play music is just like learning to speak? That sour note is your kid's version of saying "sunny" when they mean "funny." Or "wah-yu" when they mean "water" (okay, that one's a disclosure from my own toddler past).

What if you heard that clunky note as cute and endearing instead of taking it as evidence that your kid isn't talented enough to hack it in music lessons?

I wonder if I can come up with an example of another person who started with some clunky notes but ended up being proficient enough with music to win accolades, if not make a great living with their instrument. Oh, wait, I can. Me. And every other professional musician I've ever met or heard of.

Music is about expression. It's about bravery and, at first, a lot of trial and error. We have to play some wrong notes while learning how to play the right ones. Or, to make this even more clear, playing notes that aren't intended helps us learn the ones that are intended.

Instead of assuming the music lessons aren't working, what if you worked to harness the child's creativity by allowing them to be brave and make mistakes?

When I studied music history in college courses, I learned so many fascinating examples that have taken place throughout the history of classical music, jazz, and just about every type of music involving artists who "pushed the envelope" with notes that weren't supposed to be "right" for that particular genre or style. Some artists give themselves strict rules, they stick to those rules, and that's how they play. You can make beautiful music that way. Others spend a lot of time figuring out how to improvise and go "off script." Those artists can make beautiful music, too, and it's often interesting (if not groundbreaking).

Haven't you heard a musician live in concert and noticed that they didn't play or sing the tune as it was originally recorded? You can probably think of instances when you heard such a variation and thought it was pretty cool, because you had unconsciously already given that artist license to know how to "speak" the tune differently from the way they recorded it. You gave them permission to go off script, because you recognize them as a professional.

Why is it sometimes hard to extend that same license to our kids as they learn to play music? Maybe they won't be the next great recording artist, but if they stick with it, they will learn to make music that beautifully expresses themselves. What if their folks showed great joy and laughed at their "cuteness" as they learned their instrument, even when things seemed out of key? *Remember when she used to say "otay"?*

Instead of assuming the music lessons aren't working, what if you worked to harness the child's creativity by allowing them to be brave and make mistakes?

If children are shut down every time they make a mistake, will they ever have a chance to learn? What if they had never been brave enough to make mistakes when they were learning to speak?

If you're a parent who has ever felt this way, my invitation to you is to give yourself permission to laugh. Give your child permission to make all the mistakes they need to make. Guide them to the intended notes, too, when you can.

Watch the magic unfold when you give your child bravery and confidence, just like you did when they first learned to say, "It's funny, Daddy." Because life really is *sunny* when your home is filled with people learning to play or sing.

MYTH NO. 2

I Can't Support My Kid's
Music Lessons If I Can't Read
Music Myself

I remember when my oldest kid was about three years old. She joined a soccer team. In my mind, she was barely potty trained, and I was blown away that she was on a soccer team. But looking back, it was very cool. Also, it was really cute.

It took time, but I finally recognized that kids at that age aren't doing much in the way of "soccer" on the soccer field. Mostly, what's happening is that parents are clutching their coffee cups and rubbing their eyes, still getting accustomed to the idea of never sleeping again. But all of us parents came together with the same general goal: to have our kids play on the field for thirty to forty-five minutes without falling apart, crying, or throwing a tantrum. And for the kids not to do those things either.

Don't get me wrong. We all knew there was value to our kids learning about sports, gaining some socialization, and trying to follow directions from a coach. Which brings me to the funny part of this anecdote: I ended up being one of the coaches.

Why is that funny? Well, I pretty much never played a sport in my life. Up to that point, the closest thing you could call "sporting" for me would be golf, but even in that case, nobody needs to get too excited about seeing my scorecard. My qualifications for soccer coaching were that I had a pulse, and I could show up on Saturday mornings.

So there I was, supposed to be coaching a bunch of tiny kids on how to play a game I had never played myself. I explained my thin credentials to the other parents. They patted me on the back and said, "Oh, you'll do great!" Luckily, a friend of mine was helping as well, so the kids had more than one coach.

Eventually, I became a professional soccer coach, like, in two weeks, and my team won the World Cup. Twice.

That didn't happen, but I did learn some incredible things from that experience. First, I learned that I knew nothing about drills, or strategy, or even some of the rules of the game of soccer. But more importantly, I learned that it didn't matter.

I learned that the other parents weren't looking for World Cup soccer coaching. It didn't take me long to realize that what they wanted was someone who was enthusiastic and able to help rally the kids' enthusiasm too.

Second, I learned that the other parents weren't looking for World Cup soccer coaching. It didn't take me long to realize that what they wanted was someone who was enthusiastic and able to help rally the kids' enthusiasm too.

I would be lying if I said that, all of a sudden, coaching soccer became my most favorite thing to do. In fact, I'm not wired to be a good sports coach in any way. But the kids had a great time. I did relearn the lesson about stretching my own limits, and I did learn a little bit about soccer along the way.

Since the days of three-year-old soccer, the kids have grown older, the coaches have become more qualified, and the parents have become less qualified to give advice. That's good, because these are the necessary conditions for the team to get better at playing soccer. They learn strategy. They keep score! That's a plus. And the good experiences the kids had when they were three probably helped keep them "into it" long enough to learn more about the game.

I didn't have to know anything about soccer to be a good "enthusiasm coach" for the three-year-olds. And parents don't have to be maestros to play a huge role in helping their kids get the most out of music lessons.

Busted: More Cheerleader Than Coach

Do you question whether you can effectively support your kid's music lessons because you know about as much about music as I did about soccer?

You're not alone.

This is definitely one of the most common myths I've heard while running music schools for twenty years. I don't blame anyone for thinking this way, because in many ways music is in a class by itself in terms of the way people view it. Most recognize music performance as a high skill, especially since we've all experienced incredible music that really impressed us. "How do they do that? Amazing!"

But you can be assured of one thing: Music isn't some elite club that only certain people should be allowed to join.

Granted, you need to choose a music teacher who knows how to teach music. Your child won't learn much from a teacher who barely knows how to run around on the field, so to speak. But as for your role? You can relax. Grab a latte. Open a novel. Sit in on a lesson or two, if you like. But recognize that your budding young musician is in good hands if they're getting lessons at a noted music school with a track record of success in lessons, recitals, and even incentive programs that help keep the kids into it.

At our schools, we believe strongly that the more hands-off a parent is regarding the music and the more hands-on they are with the high fives and encouragement, the better students are able to grow naturally in their musical ability.

> Music isn't some elite club that only certain people should be allowed to join.

Music doesn't behave in the same way as other activities, with sports being a good example. Eventually, young soccer players grow up to play on serious teams with important records of wins and losses, but with music, there's no way to keep score. You can't count the number of repetitions that a piano warm-up will take for a student to finally get it. You can't tell somebody that if they sing a song ten times, or a hundred times, they'll finally memorize the lyrics. It's different for everyone. And you certainly can't bottle up creativity or songwriting in a way that can be measured in a number of lessons or hours.

As a parent, your role is to be your young musician's biggest cheerleader. But you don't have to be able to demonstrate any musical ability of your own in order to help your child's musical ability flourish.

As long as your kid fulfills these two basic requirements of successful music lessons, you can relax. You're doing your job.

1. Your kid shows up for their lesson, and enjoys it, most of the time.

2. Your kid is gradually getting better.

They don't have to show up for every lesson (life happens), and they don't have to enjoy every minute (there is some work involved). And they don't have to master the instrument by Thursday. It's best to measure progress after months, not hours, or even weeks.

Sometimes you can't notice a difference in ability, even when real progress is being made. This is especially true for vocal students. But if you're curious, grab a recording device and listen to recordings of how your student plays or sings, then patiently wait and record how they perform the same piece on day sixty, day ninety, and beyond. You'll likely be amazed at what can happen in a year, but you won't notice much in a day, a week, or a month.

Give it time. Relax, knowing you've done everything right by enrolling your child with fun, patient, and proficient teachers, and by consistently and enthusiastically cheering them on.

MYTH NO. 3

Music Lessons Are for People Who Want to Become Serious Musicians

I'll bet you've seen at least a little bit of the hit TV show *American Idol*, since just about everyone has.

American Idol became a sensation for many reasons. As a professional musician myself, I will admit a certain degree of schadenfreude in thinking that one of the attractions was watching people train wreck—it's the sort of thing we humans can't help but watch. (Don't get mad—that's just the truth.) But the biggest thing I noticed as a result of the popularity of *American Idol* is that there's a new level of general misunderstanding about what it takes to be successful in music.

The show went as far as to elevate the winners to fame. Before *American Idol*, similar avenues didn't exist for those artists, and I can't criticize the show for creating a platform where a very (very!) small group of people can become famous or well-known. But when we think about music success, we have to be careful not to become romanced or enchanted by this type of show.

I can't tell you how many times I've been blessed to be well paid to perform at a high-profile event where a guest casually approaches me and says, "You know, you should try out for *American Idol*." I laugh, but I realize they're paying me a compliment. They probably don't understand that there are many other ways to measure musical success besides winning, or even appearing on, a show like that.

I'm happy to say I'm able to land many good-paying gigs without ever having been noticed on television. I know lots of musicians I consider not only successful but *great*, making much more money than you might realize with their craft, and that's how many of them measure their success. But you'll never hear them on the radio.

In fact, you'll hear the work of many great musicians on the radio, and you'll never know their names. There are countless successful musicians who have made their mark as studio players or background vocalists, and their work is on a lot of the songs you like to listen to again and again.

There are so many different ways to measure success in music. Let me ask you a question: Why would you decide to enroll your son or daughter in music lessons? Was it to get them to realize success, riches, or even fame, as some of the above folks have done? If so, I caution you. Not because your kid will never get there. But because there are many other versions of "getting there" that you might never have considered.

Think about a holiday party, or some other gathering you've attended, where someone was able to sit down at a piano and play and sing a delightful tune. What value did they add to the night that never could have otherwise been added? That person's musical ability did something magical that could never have been done or replicated in any other way.

Maybe you could have played that same song on the radio or on a recording. But someone was able to do it *live* for you, and it was breathtaking. Flaws and all. That's because we all connect to real music. Real music gets to the heart of who we really are, whether we play music or not.

Busted: Music Lessons Are About Self-Expression and Play

I've highlighted some of the differences between music and sports. But one similarity I've found between the two is how parents can sometimes get caught up in the competitive nature of things.

In the early days of our music school, we decided to put together a competitive, audition-only rock band program. We had never done such a thing before. We just wanted to put kids together in rock bands, mold them together to play some shows, and have a great time. But part of our thinking was to copy some other music schools doing the same thing. We hoped it would create more of a sense of belonging and a higher sense of esteem for some of our more motivated student musicians.

But here's the problem. All the fun was immediately sucked out of the room when students had to compare themselves to others. All of a sudden, someone who was doing fine and having a great time started trying to live up to someone else's standard of what it meant to be good. Meanwhile, some of the students who weren't invited into those bands or weren't able to audition started to feel like what they were doing had no importance. And who's to say the kid who's playing a few chords and singing for the first time is any less valuable than the student who can blow you away by perfectly playing that Santana solo?

Don't get me wrong. I enjoy playing at a high level. But even I have had times when I've overemphasized "where

I am not" with my music, and it has taken all the fun out of enjoying "where I am."

One of my favorite artists is a guitar player named Steve Vai. If you've never heard him play, go now—stop reading—look him up on YouTube and listen to one of his songs. There's no arguing that he's one of the best guitarists *ever* in his category.

"Get as good as you need to get to express yourself fully."

Vai was recently asked, "How good should you get on guitar?" His answer was maybe the best I've ever heard, and nothing like I thought it would be. I thought he would say something about having discipline, or working hard, or pulling out all the stops to be the best you can possibly be. He has written books about those things, about ten-hour practice sessions and so forth. And if you aspire to become a great guitarist, you would be well served by heeding his prescriptions. But when asked how good one should get on the guitar? Steve Vai said, "Get as good as you need to get to express yourself fully."

Isn't that incredible?

He didn't say "Get so good you can win *American Idol*." He didn't say "Try to be the best singer on the entire planet, better than anyone has ever known." He didn't even say you have to practice or play for a certain amount of time. He spoke more to the internal reason people love music. Why you love it, and why you want your kid to enjoy it too.

Music is about personal expression. Think about it. If you own a variety of music, you listen to some things that might be technically incredible. But some of the best music to sing along with is actually quite simple. And that's why it's so accessible to the minds and hearts of those who never learned to play or sing.

It's a good idea to keep that in mind when it comes to the standard to which you try to hold your children. And don't think that your kid's ability to play at a certain level is what's required of you as a parent. Your best role is to find out what excites you, your son, daughter, or family member in music, and go for music lessons as a way to help draw out that excitement.

For you, does that mean playing a blistering array of notes at incredible speed and accuracy? Is that the way you want to express yourself? If so, have at it! Go for the lesson and practice regimen that can help you generate that ability. On the other hand, I've met a lot of people who love singing campfire songs, or Bob Dylan tunes, or just belting their hearts out on "Take Me Home, Country Roads." That doesn't take a Steve Vai–level of discipline, but it does take some time and effort, and it means embracing the musical journey that can take you where you want to be.

Music is a language meant to bring out the playful side of you. After all, we don't say "Let's suffer music together." We say "Let's play music together," and the word *play* is the most important.

MYTH NO. 4

Music Skill Is About Having Talent

People have had their eyes glued to their televisions for years watching people sing. Not just concerts or special performances but also popular "talent shows" like *American Idol* (as we just described). *Idol* isn't alone. Similar shows pop up constantly.

You've seen 'em. There's a panel of judges, with lots of cameras showing the concern or delight on their faces from every conceivable angle as they take in the contestants' performances. There's a studio audience, of course, waiting with bated breath for the dramatic rendering of each judge's verdict.

These shows get great ratings. That's why more and more of them keep popping up on your channel guide. But the ratings *really* soar when singers are doing their best but just don't "have it." They don't sing like professionals. You can find many popular videos on YouTube (and elsewhere) of people falling flat in front of judges, in front of studio audiences, and in front of bazillions of moms and dads and all the ships at sea.

We're fascinated by the flops, but we're even more fascinated by the climb to the top. For every season of every show, there has to be a winner. Somebody gets the crown. One of those previously unknown singers is declared to have the top talent, and the entertainment world throws its doors wide open to them. Meanwhile, we moms and dads and ships at sea go marching (sailing?) through our lives with this image of singers presented to us in ways to specifically keep us captivated and to boost the show's ratings.

After all, we're judges too. We have our own ideas about who should win, who bombed, who was robbed, and so forth. And all from the comfort of our couches. But what impressions do these images create in our minds and hearts about what really matters when it comes to singing? How does it affect our frame of reference?

Especially, how do these experiences influence people (like your teenager)? What motivations, what beliefs, what hopes, what fears end up rattling around inside us that govern how we might approach the possibility of taking singing lessons and trying to make that climb to the top, just like the contestants in this season's *American Idol*?

It's a simple answer. We start to believe that music is all about talent.

Busted: Talent Isn't Everything

What even *is* talent? I could spend the whole book on that single question. *I know talent when I see it,* you might think, and you're right. Talent is what you judge it to be. But there's that word again: *judge.*

Talent is subjective. The singer or musician you judge to be talented might not strike another person as talented at all. And that song you can't stand to listen to? The one you turn off as soon as you hear the opening chords? *Turn it off! I hate that song. I can't stand that guy.* Well, "that guy" is someone else's idea of the greatest musician on earth. That's why "that guy" is on the radio.

You could say there's no such thing as talent without judgment.

I'll prove it. Think about the last time you belted out a song in the car, all by yourself. Or the last time you sang with a group of friends (karaoke night, perhaps?). Was talent on the forefront of your mind? Was it something you cared about at all?

When we make music in a judgment-free environment—when there's nobody around who might be judging us, and we're not judging ourselves—we're free to express our music, to relax, and to enjoy the music we make.

Talent doesn't come into play at all.

If you plan to eventually become a professional musician, somebody, somewhere will have to judge your talent. (Mostly by you, I would argue.) Maybe you'll make it big (whatever that means), and maybe you won't. But either way, whether you have a life in music isn't as important as whether you have the blessing of music in your life.

And suppose somebody, somewhere *does* judge you to be talented. So what? Does that mean you'll be successful? And what even *is* success? If you're a working musician who loves playing weddings or private events, does that make you less successful or valuable—less able to make music that inspires others—than another working musician who gets picked for the Super Bowl halftime show?

And what if you're that guy who's the life of the party when he sits down at the piano and belts out a fun song, even though he never made a dime from music?

"Music skill is about having talent" might be the most important myth we can bust here. Because if you or your child are learning to sing or play an instrument, and you aren't producing a magical sound right away, and you've been influenced by judged talent shows, you might be tempted to conclude that you or your child doesn't "have it." That there isn't enough talent there to justify the pursuit of music. And if that happens, then you could lose the magical blessing of having a life filled with music.

When we make music in a judgment-free environment—when there's nobody around who might be judging us, and we're not judging ourselves—we're free to express our music, to relax, and to enjoy the music we make. Talent doesn't come into play at all.

Don't get me wrong. We all have our subjective opinions about which singers or musicians or bands are the best. We judge. As humans, we can't avoid it. But after nearly twenty years of serving communities through music lessons, I can tell you that talent doesn't mean squat when it comes to expression and enjoyment of music.

In the movie *The Natural*, the lead character, Roy (played by the late Robert Redford), is told that he has a gift, but that his gift isn't enough. That reality becomes a theme throughout the movie.

That idea is just as applicable to music as it was to Roy's gift for baseball. I've met many people who had that natural ability with music but didn't put in a lick of effort to develop it. And where do you think that leads a person? Nowhere.

On the other hand, I've met aspiring singers who couldn't carry a tune in a galvanized bucket, so to speak, but who had great passion and the dedication required to work hard and develop whatever talent they could muster and whose voice you would not be able to recognize for its "talent" a year or two after they start pursuing voice lessons. I could even name one of our students for whom this was inarguably true—and who has produced beautiful music you can stream any time.

It's a simple fact that talent isn't everything. It defies definition, just as "success" does when it comes to musical expression and enjoyment. Argue if you want, but it's hard to disagree with the fact that success and talent exist only in the heart and mind of the beholder. Music comes from the heart of self-expression; talent is only a figment of imagination driven by judgment.

We often say that music is one of the cheapest forms of therapy. Quick story: I know a guy who went to a memory care unit to sing Christmas carols with the elderly folks there who had severe memory loss. Many of them couldn't remember their own relatives. What they did remember, though? All the verses of "Hark! The Herald Angels Sing." Talk about therapy. It seems that when you lose your marbles, music is the last thing that falls out of the bag. Maybe you don't lose music at all.

You can't tell me that just because your uncle says he hasn't seen you on billboards next to stadiums that you aren't "successful" in music when you drop by a hospital to sing for sick kids. And that phenomenal band you love? The really successful hit performers? How many of them won a televised talent show?

You can't measure success only by being on billboards or a talent show winner. If you do win a talent show, congratulations! But we have to be careful when we talk about talent. Talent is only as good as the effort you put in to develop it.

If you or a loved one is enjoying music lessons and feeling true joy from learning to play an instrument or sing a favorite tune—even if it takes what you would consider a long time to get to that place of enjoyment—I say rock on with your bad self. Don't stop because someone else judges you unworthy. Keep at it until you love it yourself.

Ignore the talent myth and the head trash it piles up.

Your love of music will have nothing to do with what other people think, judge, or say. And your level of talent doesn't mean a thing.

MYTH NO. 5

If You're Not Getting It Fast,
It's Time to Give Up

Let's face it: We live in a society of drive-throughs, audiobooks, get-rich-quick schemes, and YouTube snippets that can barely keep our attention for one minute. Couple that need for speed with the previous myth about talent, and you've got yourself an interesting combination. It seems we can't keep our minds on anything for long, and we often measure success in terms of how quickly something can be accomplished.

That's often the case with music. Here we go judging again. We start buying into the head trash that presents us with this fake logic that goes something like this: You can't be successful in music if you don't have talent, and success is measured in terms of speed (fast is good, slow is failure);

therefore, if you aren't getting it fast, you don't have sufficient talent for music.

What a load. What a myth!

Are there naturals out there who have a gift and can pick up music quickly? Sure. But take a look at those fallacious statements up there. Every one of them pins its logic on the notion that something subjective is actually objective.

We've already busted some of these myths and shown how things like success and talent are purely products of a person's judgment or opinion. That's the very definition of "subjective."

It's time to give this idea of speed, or getting it fast, the same myth-busting treatment.

Busted: Objectively, There's No Such Thing As "Fast"

What does it even mean to "get it fast?"

Years ago, I knew of an a cappella group that sang everything way too fast. Getting to know the young members, I developed the impression that delivering the song quickly was a way to demonstrate to themselves that they could get through it without forgetting the words. This focus on themselves, rather than on their audience, ruined their performances. And I don't think they even knew it.

Another interesting attribute of this singing group was their tendency to want to continually learn new tunes. It was almost like they were done with a tune after they had gotten through it once without having to stop and correct something. As a result, they never took the time to perfect anything on their song list. This focus on getting through a song rather than making each performance delightful for their audience made for a group that never lived up to its potential. They won some awards (from judges!) and they made a CD, but none of the members stuck around for long. They were constantly bringing a new alto up to speed, for example.

Yes, that group was focused almost entirely on speed. And you would be hard-pressed to call them successful in music, despite their great talent, originality, and potential.

The speed with which a person "gets it," especially when it comes to music, is subjective, illusory, and irrelevant.

When it comes to learning to make music a beautiful expression of yourself and a true joy in your life, it's the journey that matters, not the destination. The people who take more time to "get it right" often "get it" far more deeply than those who rush things.

When I was working at a guitar store, my role was to sell people guitars. Easy enough for someone like me, who loves guitars. Interestingly, I found customers' most common questions had nothing to do with things like whether the instrument had a red or "sunburst" finish, whether the neck had a certain radius, how the guitar was manufactured, or even what kind of wood comprised it. I was trained to answer those technical questions, but what people most wanted to know was: What happens if this guitar leaves the store and ends up spending the rest of its life on a stand or in a case at home?

Valid question.

I found myself answering some difficult questions as part of that job. I might approach a customer to find out whether they were beginning to play, returning to the guitar after a break, or looking to upgrade their existing guitar. Invariably, the beginners would ask "How long will it take me to get good?"

It was fascinating how often I heard that question. I had a hard time answering it, especially at first, as I struggled with the subjective nature of "how long" and "get good." I stumbled through my answers. Eventually, I realized the key to busting the speed myth, as described above, and I would say, "When it comes to learning to play the guitar, it's the journey that matters, not the destination."

Here's another way to look at it. Once we've learned something well enough to feel like we get it, how long do we take to decide we should push forward to the next level? Once you've "achieved," how long until you ask, "What's next?"

Maybe that's what the a cappella singers I mentioned thought they were doing when they dumped a song into their memory hole after getting through it *once* and then immediately demanded a new arrangement to learn. But let's not confuse, as they did, "completion" with "achievement."

When it comes to learning to make music a beautiful expression of yourself and a true joy in your life, it's the journey that matters, not the destination. The people who take more time to "get it right" often "get it" far more deeply than those who rush things.

I once did an audio editing project for an Olympic gold medalist. She had put together an audio series for people to help them overcome past traumas and achieve big goals. I had a great time on the project and learned a lot in general. What stuck with me was when she described this very thing. She talked about how long it took her to ask "What's next" after she had stood on the Olympic podium and collected her medal.

She hadn't made it to the parking lot.

So as you enroll your children in music lessons, I invite you to consider how the process—*the journey*—will help them in life, no matter what sounds they end up making.

Learning how to place your hands on the keyboard, how close to your lips to keep the microphone, or how to get your saxophone reed just right, is part of an overall process that presents an ocean of value for young people.

They are learning how to learn.

There's a Russian proverb that says "Repetition is the mother of learning." And as your son or daughter proceeds on their musical journey, they'll be learning the value of repetition, of doing things over and over. The value of not just "getting it" but of taking the time to get it right.

Think about how many things in adult life are based on discipline, focus, and sheer repetition. Giving your child music lessons is one of the best ways to instill those qualities in them, which will come in handy in just a few short years.

It's not an overstatement to say that, beyond giving your child the precious gift of a music-filled life, music lessons will help them in unrelated ways you would never imagine. For one thing, a music student's school grades tend to improve after they've been studying music—especially in areas like math, where the discipline and focus they gain from music lessons really pays off. The drum student who never ends up playing with a band may nevertheless end up being an excellent putter of the golf ball, having instilled a disciplined sense of rhythm that pays dividends on the green. And almost any job your young person will later end up with will require the same qualities that will be imprinted on them by music lessons, often without their knowledge.

When the Karate Kid was forced to "wax on" and "wax off," he wasn't really learning how to wax something. He was getting a muscle memory ingrained in him that helped him master the karate moves that vanquished Cobra Kai.

But it's not just about discipline and focus. Music lessons also deliver beauty, joy, and self-expression that lasts a lifetime.

When I first picked up a guitar, and I held that pick awkwardly in my fingers, and I set forth to pluck a string and let it ring, I set something in motion for myself that never stopped ringing. The vibration of that string may have ended a few seconds later, but the vibration in my heart and soul and mind never left me. The ability to take something that is sitting still and apply my own effort to it to make music happen—it still blows my mind.

If you're afflicted by this speed myth, here's my invitation: Whenever you hear your kid honking away on the saxophone over and over again, or singing that same tune for the 1,247th time, or playing the same scales on the piano until you're sure their fingers must be bleeding . . . just smile. (Unless you have the unlikely situation where your kid really is bleeding, in which case it's not a smiling matter. Grab the first aid kit.)

Just understand that your son or daughter is on a journey they've never been on before. They're putting forth a real effort to learn, and it's requiring them to grab some skills and attributes they'll need later, no matter what they end up doing for a living. And they're gaining the ability to express themselves in a way they can't do any other way.

Don't fall into the comparison trap either. We see this with siblings, where one brother seems to get it faster than the other—even with identical twins. Relax. The world around you may be swirling at a million miles an hour, and it may be screaming that your kid should probably give up if they're not getting it faster than the kid in the next room or next door, but that's a lie. It's based on that fake logic described above. On the contrary, you're giving your kid a lifelong ability to do something that has the potential to bring them true joy. Who cares how long it takes them to unwrap that kind of gift?

*   *   *

I had many siblings growing up. One of the things that has stuck with me is something one of my sisters said as I was going off to college. "You know, the one thing we missed the most when you left the house was hearing you try to play those guitar riffs, over and over and over, through the walls."

It almost brings me to tears as I write this. My own family became accustomed to my repetition, and even to hearing how bad I was for a long time. But here we are, years later, and I can't tell you how much joy it brings me to see families overcome this speed myth and enter a world of expression and enjoyment they never thought could possibly exist.

MYTH NO. 6

No Degree, No Credibility

I'm going to make some people upset here. I promise I'm not trying to be dramatic, but some people are going to completely disagree with the way I bust this sixth myth.

As the chapter title suggests, the myth is that a music teacher without a college degree lacks credibility and that music lessons should only be offered by qualified, degreed teachers. If you're one of the people afflicted by this particular myth, I invite you to relax and ride along with me in this chapter . . . and to ask yourself why you believe this myth.

Busted: Some of the Best Teachers Don't Have the Best Degrees

When I was studying music in college, one particular teacher was everybody's favorite. Dan (not his real name, which was

Hubert, as far as you know) was an outstanding music teacher. He was also, incidentally, an outstanding musician in his own right. He could play every instrument under the sun—and not just play a little bit, but play extraordinarily.

(Dan put the lie to an old adage my grandmother used to say: "Those who can, do. Those who can't, teach." Dan could do music like nobody's business, but his real gift was teaching music.)

He was also a goofy dude, but in a way that was charming and endearing, not weird. He could tell a dumb joke about coming off a caffeine high and then smoothly transition into a complex discussion concerning ear training on intervals in scales (don't worry if you don't know what that means—neither did we, until Dan explained it). Beyond that, though, he knew our names. All our names. He learned facts about every one of the students he met, and he remembered those things, seemingly forever.

I remember seeing Dan several semesters after the class I had taken with him. He said "Hey, Stephan! How's it going with your band?" I could scarcely believe it. How did he remember my band situation, months after we no longer saw each other on a regular basis? He made me feel like the only student on campus. In reality, he made everybody feel that way. Everyone wanted a chance to talk to Dan. He was an extraordinary teacher who put everything he had into doing something he loved, and doing it well.

I later learned that, of all the music teachers on campus, Dan's "credentials" were the thinnest.

Granted, you have to have a college degree to teach at the college level. But most people who get that job have advanced degrees. People with master's degrees are often competing for jobs with PhDs. But Dan? Dan had a plain ole bachelor's degree. And he was the only music teacher on campus, as far as anyone knew, who didn't have an advanced degree.

So why was Dan the most popular music teacher on the faculty? Why did he have full classes and waiting lists for everything he offered, from coursework to individual lessons? Why, when I needed private guitar lessons to check a box for credit hours, and when I requested those lessons with Dan (naturally), was I told I couldn't take lessons with him because his wait list was out the door, down the street, and around the block?

How could this be the case with a college teacher without a high degree? How could this "underqualified" guy be the absolute best music teacher on campus, by far? Easy answer: Because Dan made it clear that it wasn't about him. It was about you.

I've been hiring music teachers for almost twenty years. Don't get me wrong, I do hire teachers with music degrees. In fact, most people who get into music mentoring do have music degrees. But as I carefully select teachers for our schools (and I do mean *carefully*), over time about one in five of the teachers I bring on board don't have degrees. I've found those teachers to be just as awesome as our degreed teachers. In some cases, they're extraordinary, just like Dan.

This one in five is a rough current estimate, as I look over our job ad responses and the pile of resumes I have on my desk right now. Lots of teachers want to work at our schools, but not all applicants make the cut. Our schools are growing rapidly, so I'm always on the lookout for great teachers. Our refined selection process and screening go way beyond background checks to help us find the Dans out there.

While I'm interviewing teachers, I'm asking myself, *Is this a person I would want my own kids to hang out with? Would I have a ton of fun learning music with this person?*

You might respond with, "Is that all it is for you, Stephan? Is it just all about the *fun?*" My answer: Yes. And that might upset some people who misunderstand the point I'm making.

"OMG, Stephan! You can't mean that! Doesn't a music teacher have to have a degree? How else could you measure their greatness? How else could a person possibly be qualified to teach my kid?"

Without an ounce of confrontation, I would respond with a question of my own. "What is it that your kid wants? I mean, really wants?"

I know the likely answer. Most kids love to learn, but they want to do something *fun* with their time. Something that doesn't feel like the kind of burden they bear with things like math and science homework.

Go to any gym and ask a personal trainer what the best workout is. Often, they'll say, "The best workout is the one you'll actually do on a consistent basis."

Kids want to learn enjoyable, fun, expressive stuff like music. Music is the workout for their heart and mind, so to speak, that they *will* do on a consistent basis. Is a PhD required to give them that kind of workout? Absolutely not.

Some of the best teachers I've ever employed did have degrees. But I don't require it. Looking at our teachers' bios, you'll see some who are working on a degree and some who don't have a degree at all, but they've all found their lane as professional musicians and music teachers. It's like some of the people I've met who have business degrees but don't know a thing about customer service (for example), because they've never done it.

Having a college degree doesn't mean that you understand how to relate to people. Don't get mad. I'm not saying that someone with a degree *can't* relate to people. But I am saying that there are music schools out there—I've seen them in action—that make a music degree their sole qualification for employment. Some of their teachers do well. Others struggle to retain any kind of student base.

Many degreed teachers take a one-size-fits-all approach to teaching music (though not all do). They insist that their students learn in the same way they themselves learned. Those teachers are often left wondering why their students aren't loving their lessons, aren't progressing, and aren't even showing up sometimes.

Imagine a kid who's on fire to learn a favorite Tom Petty tune but meets a teacher who opens a book and says, "Start on page one. Mr. Petty will have to wait. Months."

Imagine a young singer who wants to learn to nail a hit song from *Frozen* so they can have some fun and shock that stuck-up girl Tamara at the school talent show, only to be confronted with a teacher who's only trying to impress upon her the importance of following the rules.

I'm not saying only degreed teachers make these mistakes. It's complicated. All I'm saying is that we're not trying to find the best resumes out there. We're trying to find the best, most inspiring teachers.

We're looking for Dans.

* * *

Busting this myth goes right to the heart of what I truly believe.

As I write this, I have a dozen teacher interviews lined up this week. I'm constantly looking for substitutes, and as I mentioned, we're growing by leaps and bounds. Many of my teachers have waiting lists, like Dan had.

This week, I've met four teacher candidates I like who have degrees. Two other top candidates don't have degrees but have great performing and recording experience and lovely personalities. So as I decide who to hire, I keep foremost in mind what my customers—parents who enroll their kids in music lessons—really want. Beyond safety (not trivial), what parents look for is this: Is my kid having fun, and is the teacher inspiring and patient? I'm not making this up from my own opinion. I've heard it over and over from parents whose kids are taking lessons with us.

When I meet parents, my own degrees and awards never come up. I know that teaching great music lessons doesn't require a single degree of education, but it does require a degree of joy, patience, and fun that I'm sad to say many music schools don't offer. For us, what's required is that the students—the kids, their parents, and adult students—walk away from their experience with us as the stars of the show.

In our staff meetings, we always remind each other about who's the most important person in the business. It isn't me. It isn't my managers. And it isn't even my most inspiring teacher. It's you. No matter how many plaques or awards or trophies we have on the wall, or how many glowing five-star online reviews we've collected, if you aren't blown away by the fun and the joy of our schools, we've failed you.

As far as I'm concerned, we can't continue in business unless we're constantly asking ourselves if we're delighting the most important person in the business: you.

MYTH NO. 7

Changing Teachers Is Devastating

This might be the most important myth we can bust. Of all the myths about joyful and successful music lesson experiences, this myth might be the mythiest. It might myth harder than any myth ever mythed in the history of myths.

We're creatures of habit. Once we find something that works, something we like, we don't like to change. That's human nature.

It's the same with your music teacher (or your kid's music teacher). If you've found a great fit with your teacher and then life happens—the teacher moves away, experiences a tragedy, or can't keep offering lessons at the same time and day to which you've become accustomed—it kinda sucks. You don't want to change teachers. You don't want to start over. This is devastating!

Hold on. It's not devastating. In fact, no matter how much you loved that teacher, you might look back and think changing teachers was a good thing.

Busted: Changing Teachers Doesn't Mean Starting Over

Think back to the time you embarked on a new journey. Maybe you were a kid in middle school or high school and you had to meet your first new teacher at that level. Perhaps it was the time you signed up for a personal trainer at the gym, or a life coach, or a therapist . . . or even a music teacher.

You wanted something specific out of that new journey. You wanted to transform your life in some new way, to learn something you hadn't learned before. But going in, you were somewhere on the continuum between totally relaxed about meeting your new teacher or coach and totally freaked out about it. *Is this person going to be a good fit for me? What if I don't like them? What if they don't like me? What if they're mean, or strict, or teaching with a wrong style?* These are understandable, and universal, concerns.

Then you finally have your first chance to work with the person. For the sake of our example, let's say they blow you away. You hit it off. All your interactions are excellent. They get you. You get them. Sure, there are bumps in the road—there always are when the journey is new and unexplored—but you overcome the struggles and find that you're working with someone who's mentoring, coaching, teaching, or helping you in just the right way. You're so grateful.

This can happen with your (or your kid's) music teacher. I'm proud to say, at our schools, it happens a lot.

Students don't know *going in* what kind of teacher they'll have and whether there will be a good fit. But more often than not, the pairing is excellent. There are so many wonderful, qualified teachers out there. While they're all different from each other in style and outlook, chances are, there are many styles that will work just fine for you (maybe better than fine) once you get used to them.

In general, if someone's looking out for your best interest, even if they have a sense of humor or candor or approach that's different from what you might at first expect, there's likely to be a connection. Just as you have different ways of connecting with the people you meet, so does your music teacher, no matter who they are.

But going in, that's not top of mind.

We have conversations every day with families inquiring about lessons at our schools, and as a fellow parent, I understand the questions that are coming, and we take pains to train heavily on how to address those questions. *Will my child be safe here? Will my child have a good time here? Will they be able to perform music—or, if they don't want to, will they be able to decline performing? What incentives do you offer for kids to practice and get better? Will my child be allowed to learn music they really like?*

Bottom line: *When my kid gets in the car after lessons at your school and we're back into the noise of our busy lives, will there be joy in the car? Will they be happy, excited, and report that they just love their music lessons?*

Most of the time, that's exactly the case for kids who take lessons with us. In the overwhelming majority of cases, they get a teacher they like on the first try.

That's when our pickiness about teacher selection pays off. We're very particular. For that reason, we're confident that we'll assign a teacher to you that you'll like, whether it's your first music teacher or your tenth teacher over a period of years. We're going to make sure you're well taken care of.

So when we have to make a change, it can seem devastating to the student's musical journey. Nothing could be further from the truth, but we certainly understand the concern. After all, we're creatures of habit too. All of us.

We don't like the change either. We don't like having to call you up and tell you your beloved teacher is no longer available.

Over the years, we've learned that changing teachers doesn't devastate a student's musical journey, and it can actually be a great thing.

Imagine your kid going off years from now to Juilliard to audition for the finest college for music anywhere (at least, by reputation). They're in a competitive audition situation. Would you hope they had studied their entire lives with one teacher, learning music in one way, from that teacher's one perspective? Or would you imagine they would fare better if they had had multiple teachers and multiple exposures to music from many different angles?

Or maybe, years from now, your kid is the person who delights the party with their fun rendition at the piano. Would they have learned to be comfortable in a variety of settings, formal and informal, by making adjustments to their musical journey from an early age? Or would they be too anxious to share their gift with a bunch of people, some of whom might be strangers? People who might not get them, like their One Teacher did?

I don't mean to downplay the anxiety of changing music teachers, for a child or for an adult student. It isn't just because we're creatures of habit that we don't look forward to making changes like this. But remember how you felt before you met that departing teacher you loved so much, with whom you hit it off so spectacularly? Going in, you didn't know you would be so lucky. You were delightfully surprised. Going in, you had the same anxieties you feel now. But guess what? You're likely to be delightfully surprised again.

There's also something powerful about teaching kids at an early age to roll with changes. Nothing is more certain than that they'll face many changes in their lives. The adults who do best in life may well be the people who learned early on that things like changing music teachers aren't at all devastating.

On the contrary, a new teacher doesn't mean you're starting over from square one. Your new teacher wouldn't let that happen. They're going to be interested in how you've progressed so far, and they'll have a new, fresh perspective on how you can take the fun, the joy, and the self-expression to whatever the next level is for you.

You won't be starting over at the bottom of the Musical Ladder (a cool incentive program our teachers employ to help students get engaged with learning music). Your new teacher will quickly help you determine how high you've already climbed and how you can keep moving higher.

* * *

Changing teachers presents an opportunity to increase your rate of learning, and even to improve your musical journey experience. At this point, I've learned from thirteen guitar teachers, eight voice teachers, and a variety of piano teachers. Every one of them left me with something special—even the few with whom I didn't connect. Looking back, I can say it helped me understand myself better to realize I didn't connect with everybody, and to ask myself why that was the case.

At our schools, we would love to help you find that One Teacher and stick with them forever. But we know that's not realistic. So instead, when change does come, we work hard to make sure that it isn't devastating. Change is a refreshing opportunity to add a beautiful new square to the crazy quilt that is your musical journey to joy.

You never know. The best music teacher you'll ever have may well be that next new person you've yet to meet.

<h1 style="text-align:center">MYTH NO. 8</h1>

All Lesson Studios Are the Same

I asked to use the restroom, and the experience was an eye-opener.

You see, I had been walking around a big retail music store, looking for a new digital piano, for some time. I was impressed with how clean and well laid out everything was. I was excited to make a purchase from this well-managed business.

Before I could decide on a purchase, nature called, and I asked to use the restroom. I was directed to the back of the store, behind a giant black curtain. Back I went.

I literally pulled back the curtain on this store, and my entire impression of the business changed. Out on the floor, everything was clean and tidy. Behind that curtain, everything was cluttered. It looked like the set of *Sanford and Son* back there (look it up). I chose my steps carefully, to avoid tripping, and made my way to the restroom.

It was even worse in there. I'm talking truck stop restroom conditions. My nose confirmed what my eyes suggested: the floor, the fixtures, none of it had been cleaned in some time. I got back in front of the curtain as quickly as I could. I felt a sense of urgency to get back to the travel-size bottle of hand sanitizer I keep in my vehicle.

Okay, I did buy the piano. But I no longer felt the enthusiasm for the transaction that I would have felt if I hadn't seen behind the curtain.

I'm not saying everything has to be perfect in your place of business. We have storerooms at our schools—that's unavoidable—but even those are way tidier than what I found behind that big black curtain, and no customers ever see our storerooms. They certainly don't have to step around clutter to get to our restrooms (which, by the way, are spotless).

We've learned that *where* you're learning music impacts *how* you learn it.

I believe that the condition of your business's physical space is part of the promise you're making to your customers. We have our act together. We're professionals. We will take good care of you in every way we can. If your joint is junky or dirty, your customers (and potential customers) might be justified in wondering what else isn't under control in your business.

There's another part to this myth, though. Many parents wonder why they need to take their kid to a music school at all. "Can't you send a teacher to our house?" we've been asked, several times. The answer is always no, for good reasons.

We've learned that *where* you're learning music impacts *how* you learn it.

Busted: Location, Location, Location— It Matters

You can probably find someone who will come to your house and teach your kid in your living room. You can find people who will give music lessons in the park, at a friend's house, at their own house, or even at a pub where people drink beer and strum along. (Yes, that's a real thing, believe it or not.)

It's not impossible to learn music that way. But it's not the experience we offer our families. You can take a correspondence course to learn how to groom dogs, ink tattoos, or hit golf balls—but I wonder how good at doing those things you would get. I wonder how those experiences would compare with having an expert show you, step-by-step, how to do it.

We've chosen a different lane, and it's where our families want to be. We offer a clean, safe, well-organized, fun environment where parents can rely on a consistent, repeatable experience. You can relax in our lobby, reading a book or checking your email. Meanwhile, the little kids can enjoy our play area while their older brother or sister learns to shred a favorite guitar riff in one of the tidy, well-organized lesson rooms.

You can always see into our lesson rooms, on our security cameras or through the glass side panels on every door.

Check out the smile on your daughter's face as she runs her fingers around the piano. Feel free to step in and observe the lesson, any time you want. Or, if this is the one hour you have to yourself, you can go out to your car and take a nap, secure in the knowledge that your kid is safe and happy. (One of our dads does this regularly.)

(One more plus, and I won't say it happens all the time, because I don't want to put pressure on my expert bakin' wife, but a lot of the time, there are delicious homemade cookies in the lobby. Help yourself! We know you didn't sign up for cookies, but we also know it's an appealing addition.)

We've found that folks are fine with an older building (call it "charm"), as long as the space is clean, well laid out, properly equipped, and staffed with happy, caring people. As long as everybody's comfortable, from Mom and/or Dad to the student to the toddler sibling, I feel we've provided the right space for optimal learning.

Meanwhile, our thoroughly vetted professional instructors enjoy a consistent, repeatable teaching experience too. They spend their time teaching, not driving from lesson location to lesson location. They have time-tested curricula to pull from and endless opportunities to bring their own teaching creativity into their work. They use the Musical Ladder system with their students, which helps them monitor and encourage each student's individual progress and reward milestones. They never have to step around clutter (or bar stools) to get to their "work stations," which they can rely on having the right equipment for the job.

They also have office staff who answer the phones and do their best to find new students for them. They don't have to advertise or sell their services. We do that for them. They can focus on the part of the job they love best: teaching and inspiring folks with music.

As previously detailed, we're picky about the teachers we employ. We take the time to get to know as much as we reasonably can about them. Many who make it to the first interview don't make it to the second. Then there are background checks and other things we do to vet candidates, and not everyone makes it past those screens. Then we train, train, and train them to provide every family with the best possible music lesson experience, every time. We want to make sure, as much as possible, that a teacher candidate is a good fit for our school.

We do this because we're looking for the best professional teachers who will stick around as long as possible. No teacher sticks around forever, but many of our teachers stay with us for a long time. That's because we also take pains to make sure we are a good fit for them. Are they okay with the commute to our location? Are they comfortable building their practice over time, even one student at a time in some cases? Does the schedule we need them to keep work within their lives? We want our teachers to be excellent, of course, but we also want to make sure they're happy here. And I'm pleased to report that, for the overwhelming majority, that's the case.

*   *   *

We know you have a choice, and it's like a lot of other choices in our modern lives. Some people love working at home, while others appreciate having the separation between work and private life that only comes by having a workplace to which they drive. Some folks might do okay working out at home with YouTube, but others much prefer to go to a real gym (and work out with a pro trainer). There are people who like to use the Zoom platform to catch up with friends, but many prefer to meet them at a coffee shop.

Location matters. The families we serve vastly prefer the learning spaces we've worked hard to provide for their students—safe, clean, spacious, fully equipped spaces staffed with the finest teachers our market has to offer.

Come take a tour of our school. You might prefer this location for your child's musical inspiration too.

MYTH NO. 9

You Have to Read Music, Of Course

Let's return to the previous scenario of your kid learning to talk, to illustrate the importance (or not) of reading music. When your kid started saying their first words, it was great because it was cute. Your daughter might have said things like "baba" instead of bottle. She might have mispronounced someone's name or even repeated a full sentence, though not quite in the right way. But it was always cute.

We parents would laugh but also then help them pronounce the word or sentence correctly. (Even my parents endured my learning to say "May I please have a drink of water?" Folks, if you're reading this, I've almost got it.)

We love our kids. We recognize that they're learning. Learning to speak any language takes time and effort and a lot of encouragement. Over time, after mistakes and immersion and encouragement, we tend to get it right.

That's how it is with the language of music too.

If you stick with your musical journey long enough, at some point you'll probably learn to read the language you've been "speaking" through your instrument for some time. You'll simply want to take that next step.

On the other hand, some musicians you would consider "accomplished" never felt the need to learn to read a score. That didn't stop them, and it doesn't have to stop you or your child.

It's a myth to suggest you have to read music in order to enjoy playing or singing it.

Busted: No, You Don't Have to Read Music, At Least Not Right Now

It's true—you don't have to read music. Even expert sight-readers generally didn't start out by learning to read music before they grabbed an instrument or microphone and started playing or singing. Music is a language, much like any other. And only after first learning to speak a language do we start to learn how to read it.

Let me point out, too, that there are some languages spoken on this earth that don't have a written form at all. The folks who use those languages seem to communicate just fine with each other.

The process of learning the language of music tends to follow a predictable path. It starts with experimentation, which includes lots of mistakes, lots of squeaks and squawks, and lots of pitchy notes—and family members who decide to go sit in a different room. There are broken guitar strings. There are broken bow hairs.

There are often hours of mild frustration punctuated by moments of sheer triumph along the way.

At the end of this path, the music student gets to a point where they can play or sing a song just like the original, or even with their own added creative twists. But there are no shortcuts. It takes time, patience, and trial and error. The amount of time it takes varies wildly from musician to musician.

> Music is a language, much like any other. And only after first learning to speak a language do we start to learn how to read it.

Young Mozart nailed it quickly. Many others, including Jimi Hendrix, John Coltrane, and Eric Clapton, took years. Leonard Cohen didn't even start on his musical learning path until he was thirty-three.

Is Stevie Ray Vaughan one of your favorite guitarists? (If not, why not?) It might surprise you to learn that he never played music by reading it. And he's not alone. A good handful of the musicians you love to hear never learned to read music at all. They sure learned to "speak" the language pretty well, though.

It seems that playing music and reading music are only somewhat and sometimes related. For some really good musicians, those two things didn't turn out to be related at all.

Now, I don't mean to upset the musical purists out there. I can already hear (hear?) one of my guitar professors shaking his head. Granted, when I went to college for music, I had to learn to read music and to demonstrate that I could sight-read the score as I played piano or guitar or sang. Before that, though, I had already played many gigs, written many songs, and been paid to complete recording projects that have been played all over the world.

I had done all that stuff before I learned to read music. I guess I could already speak it okay.

If you're laboring beneath a steaming pile of this particular myth, let me give you some other points to consider. You never followed along on the printed score when you attended a concert, and you never will. None of the albums, CDs, cassette tapes (hi, Dad), or song downloads you buy include a score. You learned to listen to English, then to speak it, and only then to read and write it. That's how every musician learns the language of music, in that same order. When you sing in the car or in the shower, there's no score handy. And you wouldn't look at it if there were.

When a kid first sits down at a piano keyboard and pounds away with their chubby little fingers, they're not reading a musical score, are they? They're enjoying themselves, hearing the sounds they're able to make. Some even plunk out something close to a melody, after some trial and error. For most, though, it's "jazz." (A little joke thrown in there for my professors, if they're reading. But I digress.)

And unless you're a stage actor at callbacks, you're not reading the words you speak every day. Those come from your mind and heart. It's the same for the young guitarist (maybe your own kid) who just learned to nail a favorite tune without having yet learned to read the score.

* * *

All that said, it's not like your new music student will never learn to read music. The instructors at our schools certainly have great methods for teaching folks how to read the language. In fact, there are some instruments for which I would suggest that learning to read, at least a little, is important as you learn to play. But it's a flat-out myth that you have to be able to read music to enjoy it.

You would probably agree, based on your own experience growing up, that learning to read English was a lot harder than learning to speak it. Same with music. Lots of synapses have to fire in the head of a musician to allow them to see black dots on a piece of paper (or screen) and play those notes with the correct rhythm, pitch, inflection, and duration. So it takes time to train that gray matter. But what a blessing it is when a musician finally learns to do it. I imagine it's a lot like the blessing you experienced when you were first able to read a book you enjoyed.

If you are (or your child is) struggling to learn to read music, struggle on. It's worth it. It takes your enjoyment of music, and your ability to express yourself through playing or singing, to an even higher level. Encourage effort. Celebrate accomplishments. That's what our instructors do, and that's why so many of our students stick with their musical journeys long enough to learn to read the language of music.

A lot of the enjoyment anyone can get from music has nothing to do with reading it. Believing otherwise is pure mythology.

MYTH NO. 10

A Few Lessons Should Do It

I can't tell you how proud I am of my wife, for many reasons. One of those is how, after delivering three children, she has become a great long-distance runner. Inspired by her example, I'm learning to be a runner myself.

Technically, I've known how to run since elementary school, when gym class came around each week. Running is one thing. Being a runner is another. What I mean by "learning to be a runner" is that I'm learning what it takes for me to run on purpose, on a consistent basis, for exercise. And I have to admit: I don't really like it. I'm one of those people who's more of an "I'm glad I ran" guy than an "I'm glad to be running" guy. There's a big difference there.

I do my runs because I know it's good for me. It's good to discipline myself to do it. Also, I run because of my deep love for ice cream. Am I right?

But for running to count as a health-maintenance practice, I know I have to do it consistently, even though I'm generally never stoked to get out there and run. My body neither knows nor cares today that I ran a half-marathon or two over the past few years. It doesn't care that I totaled six miles last week or that my intention is to put in a few more miles today. For my running to count toward my overall health regimen, my cardiovascular system requires that I do it on a regular basis.

It will take more than a few lessons to develop the learning habit necessary for a life blessed with music. You can't just stick a toe in the water. You have to dive in and give it time.

I'm slowly getting better at being a runner. A little smoother, a little faster, a little farther from home before turning around, each day. As a result, I can do a lot more than I could when I first started learning to be a runner several months ago.

Like many people, I've tried other ways to get back in shape after letting myself get a bit out of condition. I'm one of many people you probably know who used to do the old New Year's resolution thing—join a gym right after Christmas with the full intention that "this is the year," only to find by about February that I'm dropping by the gym on occasion, and by March, not at all.

Running works better for me. Remember, the best workout is the one you'll actually do. And since running is something my wife and I can do together (well, by together, I mean with me at least fifty to one hundred yards behind, for now), it's something I will do. Even if I don't love it for its own sake.

My business has brought to my attention that there are many people out there who take up music lessons with the same sort of attitude I had when I bought my annual January gym membership. Maybe it's a parent who gets their kid that coveted guitar for Christmas and enrolls them in lessons to start in January. Maybe it's an adult who tells themselves "I want to get back to playing the bass guitar" and signs up for lessons after Christmas. Some of these folks stick with it. Some, perhaps persuaded by Myth No. 10 "a few lessons should do it" or even Myth No. 5 "if you're not getting it fast, it's time to give up" don't make it to the second month of lessons.

They've been made to believe that "just a few lessons" will do it for them. It's a myth. Just as it would be a myth if I had told myself that one January at the gym or running one mile would make me a prime physical specimen.

Busted: You Have to Give It Time

Your child can learn to play the guitar, or the piano, or whatever instrument they asked for and got from Santa. You can get back to slappin' the bass well enough to gig with a band. But it will take more than a few lessons to develop the learning habit necessary for a life blessed with music. You can't just stick a toe in the water. You have to dive in and give it time.

The thing about learning music is that you do get better, gradually, over time. Just like it took time for me to gradually get better at being a runner. How much time? That will depend on you. Your willingness and ability to immerse yourself in this new language. Your brain. Your dexterity. Your discipline. Really, it all depends on the heart you have for it.

At our music schools, we offer lessons on a month-to-month basis. We don't want to force anyone to show up for lessons because they have a long-term contract. That said, we definitely encourage new students and their families to give it time.

Did your daughter beg Santa for a keyboard because that stuck-up girl Tamara has one, and she's jealous of Tamara, but she doesn't really have that much interest in learning to play the thing? I'm not telling you what Santa should bring your kid for Christmas, but it might be nice to learn what your daughter's real motivations are. It could be that she'll become the next Chopin, regardless of Tamara envy (or lack of it). But if it's a couple of months later and she's really not into coming for her lessons, that will be sad. We'll do everything possible to help light that spark of musical inspiration for her, but in the end, she'll have to have the heart to learn this wonderful new ability.

The dude who tells me as he's signing up for lessons in January, that this is the year he's going to get back into form as a gigging bass player? If we get to about March and he's wanting to drop out, I'll sit down with him and say, "Okay, so you bought into myth number five and thought this would happen overnight. But let me ask you: Aren't you playing more than you were before? Aren't you digging that? Don't you think it will happen, if you just give it more than a few lessons?"

When I meet our new students, young or adult, I always encourage them to give it time. If it's something you really want to do and you approach it with the right stick-to-it attitude, you *will* get better over time. It might shock you to look back a year later and see (or hear) the progress you've made. But don't give it three or four lessons. Give it three or four months. While you're at it, give it six months. Or a year.

I always encourage parents to tell their kids they will have to stick with lessons for at least six months. The smart parents say things to their January-eager young'uns like, "So that means this summer, you still have to be going to your lessons and practicing. That's the deal you're making. Is that clear?"

Smart parents like this know that, in six months, their kid will not make it to every lesson, and they won't practice every single day. But they also know that, if the heart is there, progress will be made in half a year. Often, it's *great* progress.

Everybody's different. Your child might pick things up quickly. Many of our young students do. But there isn't a shortcut. It's always going to be a gradual process, no matter what "gradual" is for one individual as opposed to another.

You can't cram for a song. Believe me, I've tried. Back in college, when the professor assigned us a piano midterm, he made it clear that we would have to practice every single day, if only briefly, to be able to perform the material well by the middle of the term. He was right. Yours truly, along with maybe a couple of other students, thought I could cram for the midterm by blowing off practice until a few days before and then playing my fingers off. When I fell flat, I learned something valuable about the *gradual* power of disciplined, regular practice and lessons.

Our students who really get what they came to lessons for are the ones who give it time. They came into the process knowing it would take several months, or even years. They knew at some point that the learning process would ebb and flow, that there would be times when they fell out of the practice habit for a bit or life interposed with their intention to get to their lessons. But if they have the heart for it, they dive back in, and eventually they catch up and run ahead of where they were before the ebb.

(It's also a happy bonus that developing this "dive back in" mentality pays dividends in other areas of life, like school and careers, and it's a mentality that serves a person well for the entirety of their life.)

* * *

Here's the bottom line: What is the version of yourself, or your child, that you want to meet a year after starting on the musical journey? What resolutions do you want to make (or not make *again*) when New Year's rolls around? What songs do you want to be glad you didn't neglect to learn? What music do you want to hear in your home every day?

Give it time. It's a gradual, but worthwhile, process.

CONCLUSION

Don't Let Busted Myths Keep
Music Out of Your Life

There you have it: Ten myths that keep *some other* people from enjoying the blessing and expression of music in their lives. But for you? These myths are flat-out busted. They will not keep that blessing from you and your family.

I don't know a lot of things. But I know a lot about music lessons after nearly two decades of running a music lesson business. I know that music lessons, particularly at our music schools, will help you get that blessing into your life. I hope you found the reading valuable.

I know plenty of people who simply enjoy pulling out their guitar once in a while to sing with friends. And that's just as beautiful for them as opening for Joe Satriani might have been for me, or someone else. So find your lane. Find what works for you. Know that when you have an instrument in your hands—or even just your own enthusiastic voice—you are in possession of something truly beautiful, and potentially very powerful.

I hope you find great inspiration in music.

And I hope you've enjoyed riding along with me as we busted these myths. Maybe you can relate to all of them, or maybe to just a few. But hopefully, something in these pages resonates with you. And if there's something holding you back—that's okay. That's exactly why I wrote this book: to help you bust the myths that could keep music out of your life.

I would love the honor of an opportunity to help you further. If you have questions or would like more information about our award-winning music schools, please don't wait to contact us.

Littleton School of Music

(303) 972-7625

www.littletonmusiclessons.com

Parker Music Academy

(303) 550-1081

www.parkermusicacademy.com

ABOUT THE AUTHOR

Stephan Hume appeared on the hit MTV show *Made* and is recognized as an international expert on youth music education. He is a renowned guitarist, singer, recording artist, and entertainer.

Stephan's passion for music and education led him to start Littleton School of Music in 2006. Today, Stephan leads the bright and talented staff of Littleton School of Music and Parker Music Academy as they help students do more than just play music.

His desire is for students and staff to bust through the myths of what it means to enjoy music lessons and to get on with having fun!